God With Her

A Study of Courageous Women in the Bible

By Laura Noel

Inspired Forever Books
Dallas, Texas

God With Her

A Study of Courageous Women in the Bible

Copyright © 2020 Laura Noel

All rights reserved, including the right of reproduction in whole or in part in any form without prior written permission, except in the case of brief quotations embodied in critical reviews and certain other noncommercial uses permitted by copyright law.

Inspired Forever Books™

"Words with Lasting Impact"

Dallas, Texas

(888) 403-2727

https://inspiredforeverbooks.com

Library of Congress Control Number: 2020915178

ISBN 13: 978-1-948903-40-0

Printed in the United States of America

Disclaimer: We truly hope that this Bible study helps all who read it in their quest for a better understanding of and relationship with God. To that end, we make no representations or warranties of any kind, express or implied, as to the use of this information or content.

Table of Contents

Introduction v

Week 1
From Outcast to Righteous: The Story of Rahab..................................1

Week 2
A Courageous Leader: The Story of Deborah.....................................7

Week 3
A Noble Woman from a Foreign Land: The Story of Ruth..................13

Week 4
A Wise Woman in the Desert: The Story of Abigail...........................19

Week 5
An Unnamed Hero: The Story of the Shunammite Woman.................25

Week 6
A Courageous Queen: The Story of Esther.......................................31

Week 7
Mother of the Messiah: The Story of Mary.......................................37

Week 8
Courageous Women Who Walked with Jesus....................................43

A Final Word..51
#Passages...53
Bibliography..55
About the Author...57

Introduction

"Do Not Be Afraid"

Perhaps no book has suffered from more misconceptions than the Bible. Some think that the Bible is a book of rules in which God says "don't do this" or "don't do that" simply because he wants to spoil our fun. But this could not be further from the truth. Have you ever actually thought about what the most frequent command is in the Bible? Don't sin? Love your neighbor? Be nice? While all of these are important, the most frequent command in the Bible is "Do not be afraid."[1] Well, you might say to yourself, that is much easier said than done. True. But I believe that God is telling us that he will give us the courage to do what we need to do if we will only trust in him. The bottom line is that we are not alone; God is with us. We can be courageous women. You see, courage is not the absence of fear; it is moving forward and doing what needs to be done *in spite of fear*. Webster's Dictionary defines courage as, "brave, bold, daring, hardy to encounter difficulties and dangers." Did you catch that last part? Brave or hardy *in the face of difficulty and danger*.

This brings us to another common misconception about the Bible, and it concerns women. Many people think that God does not like women, or they believe that women are portrayed negatively in the Bible. This too could not be further from the truth. In fact, this is where the two misconceptions converge. There are many stories of courageous women throughout the Bible. Women who stared straight into the face of

---

[1] N. T. Wright, *Following Jesus: Biblical Reflections on Discipleship* (Grand Rapids, MI: William B. Eerdmans Publishing Company, 1994), 68.

danger, and in some cases death, but stepped out in courage to do what needed to be done. Were they afraid? Possibly, but they weren't going to let that stop them. The key passage for this study will be: "Be strong and courageous. Do not be afraid; do not be discouraged, for the Lord your God will be with you wherever you go" (Joshua 1:9). The key to the strength and courage of these women was that God was with them.

Before we get started, I would like to take a moment to explain the format of this study. Some of you may have done more Bible studies than you can count; great! I hope you enjoy this one. Some of you might be doing your very first Bible study; welcome! I hope you find an insatiable appetite for God's Word. When I first started Bible study almost twenty years ago, I didn't even have a Bible! A friend loaned me her husband's Bible, an NIV, and I have been hooked ever since! My goal was to write a Bible study that was easy to follow and didn't require a heavy time commitment. Each of the eight lessons is followed by just eight questions.

Although it was many years ago, I remember one of my first Bible studies. The author had jumped right into the study without providing any context or historical background. I found myself lost and confused, trying to figure out who was who and what was going on. For this reason, I have written lesson introductions and provided study notes to give further insight. Please keep in mind that these weekly introductions are just brief summaries to set the stage—not capture the entire story. Scripture passages have been provided in case you wish to do further reading (and I would encourage you to do so). I have also provided encouraging hashtag Scripture passages at the end of each "Reflection" for you to look up. No time? No worries! The hashtag passages have been written out for you at the end of this study. The Bible translation I have used in this study is the NIV, but any Christian Bible is just fine.

Okay, time to get started. Over the next eight weeks, we will be taking a look at some women whose courage seems to jump off the pages of Scripture. Women who were courageous in a culture that severely marginalized women. Women who knew what needed to be done and courageously stepped out in faith. Fear was not going to stop them, and it's not going to stop us. Let's go!

Week 1

From Outcast to Righteous:
The Story of Rahab
(Joshua 2:1-24, 6:17-25;
Matthew 1:5; Hebrews 11:31; James 2:25)

The first courageous woman we will be studying is Rahab. Now, before we jump into our study, a little background information is in order. We need to set the stage.

For a better understanding of Rahab's story, we must briefly go back to where it all started in the pages of Genesis—to God's covenant promises to Abraham. God said to Abraham, "Leave your country, your people and your family and go to the land I will show you" (Genesis 12:1). Abraham did as God had asked and left his home in Ur (modern day Iraq), along with his wife, Sarah, and his nephew Lot, and traveled to the land of Canaan. Now, Abraham and Sarah were well along in years and had no children, but God promised Abraham, "I will surely bless you and make your descendants as numerous as the stars in the sky and as the sand on the seashore. Your descendants will take possession of the cities of their enemies, and through your offspring all nations on earth will be blessed" (Genesis 22:17-18). However, this was not God's only promise to Abraham. God also revealed to Abraham, "Know for certain that for four hundred years your descendants will be strangers in a country not their own and they will be enslaved and mistreated there. But I will punish the nation they serve as slaves, and afterward they will come out with great possessions" (Genesis

15:13-14; Acts 7:6). In fulfillment of God's promise, Abraham and Sarah had a son, and they named him Isaac. Isaac eventually married and had twin sons, Esau and Jacob. The covenant promise passed along from Abraham to Isaac and then to Isaac's son Jacob. Jacob had twelve sons whose descendants formed the nation of Israel. In fact, God changed Jacob's name to Israel (Genesis 32:28). Due to a famine in Canaan, Jacob, his sons, and their families packed up and moved to Egypt.

Time passed, and the Israelites greatly increased in number. Feeling threatened by the vast population of Israelites, a paranoid Pharaoh oppressed the Israelites, forcing them into slavery (Exodus 1:8-11). God heard the cries of his people, and he called Moses to lead the Israelites out of slavery and into the Promised Land (Canaan).

Do you see the circle here? Abraham left his home and went to Canaan; his descendants went to Egypt; and then they were lead back to Canaan—to a land that had been theirs in the first place.

The Israelites had been in Egypt for 430 years (Exodus 12:40). The Exodus from Egypt is believed to have occurred in 1446 B.C. (1 Kings 6:1). While journeying to the Promised Land, the Israelites rebelled against God, going so far as to make a golden calf to worship (Exodus 32:1-4). Because of their rebellion, God punished that generation of Israelites, and they wandered in the desert for forty years on a journey that should have taken only eleven days (Deuteronomy 1:2-3). During that time, the rebellious generation passed away (Numbers 14:34); the only exceptions were Caleb and Joshua (Numbers 14:38).

Sadly, Moses died before entering the Promised Land, and Joshua became the leader of the Israelites (Joshua 1:1-5). It would be Joshua who would lead the Israelites across the Jordan River and into the Promised Land. But like any great leader, Joshua would need to scope out the land first. Jericho was about seven miles from the Jordan River, and the city was surrounded by a great wall. Joshua knew he would be entering a heavily fortified city. Seeking strategic information, he secretly sent two spies into the city of Jericho (Joshua 2:1). The stage has now been set, and it is here, in the second chapter of the book of Joshua, that we meet a courageous young woman named Rahab.

Please read Joshua 2:1-24.

1. Joshua sent two spies to go look over the land. In **Deuteronomy 8:6-9**, how is the Promised Land described?

2. It is interesting to note here that aside from Joshua, Rahab is the only one mentioned by name. The spies were not named and neither was the king or any of his men. How does **Joshua 2:1** describe Rahab? (See study note 1 for further insight.)

3. Do you think it was a coincidence that the spies "just happened" to choose Rahab's house? Explain your answer.

4. Rahab lied to protect the two spies (2:4-5). Do you think it was acceptable for her to lie? Read **Exodus 1:15-21** for further insight.

5. What do you think could have happened to Rahab if the king had found out she had lied to him and hidden the Israelite spies? Why then did she do it (2:9-10)?

6. Rahab paved the way for the Israelites to conquer Jericho. How would the Israelites protect her and her family (2:17-19)?

7. Rahab risked her life to protect the spies. She affirmed that the land of her people should be given to the Israelites. She acknowledged the miraculous things God had done for his people. She professed her faith in the God of the Israelites and rejected her Canaanite gods. (See study note 2

for more information on Canaanite gods.) Please read **Hebrews 11:31** and **James 2:25**. What is Rahab commended for in these two passages?

_____
_____
_____
_____
_____

8. Despite Rahab's important role, she is not mentioned again in the Old Testament. What do we learn about Rahab in **Matthew 1:5-6**?

_____
_____
_____
_____
_____

Study Notes

1. "Some commentators have sought to show that the Hebrew word normally translated prostitute should be interpreted as innkeeper when it refers to Rahab. The Hebrew text, however, provides no basis for translating the word in any but its usual sense. Other commentators have agreed that Rahab was a prostitute but have rejected the idea that she was a hero. Still others argue that Rahab entrapped or manipulated the spies. However, such interpretations seem to reflect the readers' opinions of prostitutes, foreigners, or women more than they reflect the textual evidence. In any case, the New Testament authors clearly understood Rahab as both a prostitute and a hero."[2]

---

2   Carolyn Pressler, *Joshua, Judges, and Ruth* (Louisville, KY: Westminister John Knox Press, 2002), p. 24.

2. The Canaanites worshiped about seventy gods and goddesses, including Baal (the storm god), Yam (the sea god), and Mot (the god of death), to name a few. "The Canaanites, and eventually many Israelites and Judeans, worshiped the storm god Baal—the one who brought fertility to the land. In addition, they worshiped the sex goddess Asherah. Numerous fertility figurines have been found in archaeological excavations in Israel. From some of the texts found at Ugarit (a city in Syria) we know that Canaanite worship could include ritual dancing and the cutting and slashing of one's body—which is exactly what the 450 prophets of Baal and the 400 prophets of Asherah did on Mount Carmel (1 Kings 18:25-29)."[3]

Reflections: Rahab, a Canaanite prostitute, shunned by society, courageously stepped out in faith and ended up a member of the royal line of David and an ancestor of the Messiah! Even though Rahab said "a great fear" has fallen on us (Joshua 2:9) and "our hearts melted and everyone's courage failed" (Joshua 2:11), she did not let fear keep her from doing what needed to be done, and God richly blessed her. *#Deuteronomy 1:21*

---

[3] Halley, Henry H., *Halley's Bible Handbook* (Grand Rapids, MI: Zondervan, 2000), p. 247.

Week 2

A Courageous Leader:
The Story of Deborah
(Judges 4:1-24)

Next up on our study of courageous women: Deborah. Once again, before we go any further, some background information is needed.

Thanks to Rahab's help, the spies' mission was a success, and Joshua triumphantly led the Israelites into the Promised Land. After Joshua's death, the period of the Judges would begin, and it is in this period that the story of Deborah unfolds. The period of the Judges began with the death of Joshua and ended with the coronation of Saul, Israel's first king. However, there is some debate about how much time elapsed between these two events. Most scholars are in agreement that the monarchy began under Saul in 1051 B.C., and the date of Joshua's death is generally believed to have been around 1350 B.C. Given these dates, the period of the Judges would have been about three hundred years.

With the death of Joshua, there was a leadership vacuum, and the twelve tribes of Israel acted independently of each other. "In those days Israel had no king; everyone did as he saw fit" (Judges 17:6). These were dark, difficult times. Israel was at one of its lowest points, and sadly, much of it was of Israel's own making. You see, while the Israelites had triumphantly entered the Promised Land, they had been commanded by God to drive out the pagan nations that were living there (Deuteronomy

7:1-8); however, they failed to do so. The Israelites chose instead to live among the pagan nations, and as a result, many of them began to take on the behaviors of those nations, including idol worship. Judges 2:10-12 states: "After that whole generation had been gathered to their fathers *(meaning that generation had died)*, another generation grew up, who knew neither the Lord nor what he had done for Israel. The Israelites did evil in the eyes of the Lord and served the Baals *(pagan gods)*. They forsook the Lord, the God of their fathers, who had brought them out of Egypt. They followed and worshiped various gods of the peoples around them." Interesting to note, the phrase, "the Israelites did evil in the eyes of the Lord," is repeated seven times in the book of Judges.

The Israelites were invaded multiple times by the surrounding nations: Moabites (Judges 3:12-20); Canaanites (Judges 4-5); Midianites (Judges 6-9); Ammonites (Judges 10:6-11:40); and the Philistines (Judges 14-16). As Judges 2:16-17 states: "Then the Lord raised up judges, who saved them out of the hands of these raiders. Yet they would not listen to their judges but prostituted themselves to other gods and worshiped them." There are twelve judges mentioned in the book; however, these were not the only judges to serve the Israelites, as noted in 1 Samuel Chapter 8.

Now, let's get back to our courageous woman. Deborah was Israel's only female judge. Judges Chapter 4 opens with the Israelites having been brutally oppressed by the Canaanites for twenty years. But what were the Israelites to do? The Canaanites had a superior military force with nine hundred iron chariots (4:13), and Deborah herself would later explain that "war came to the city gates and not a shield or spear was seen among the forty thousand in Israel" (5:8). Clearly, the Israelites would be no match for the Canaanite army, but Deborah knew that God was with them and that it was time for her to take action!

Please read Judges Chapter 4.

1. What do we learn about Deborah in 4:4-5?

2. In verse 6, whose command was it to go into battle with the Canaanites? How did Barak respond in verse 8?

3. Do you think God was pleased with Barak's response? Do you think his response was culturally acceptable? Explain your answer.

4. How did Deborah encourage Barak in verse 14? According to verse 15, who "routed Sisera and all his chariots and army by the sword"? (See study note for further insight.)

5. Abandoning his army, Sisera fled on foot to the tent of a woman named Jael. Why do you think Sisera thought he would be safe in Jael's tent?

6. How did Jael handle the situation?

7. How would you describe Deborah's leadership? Compare her leadership style with that of Barak and Sisera.

8. Outside of the book of Judges, Deborah is not mentioned anywhere in Scripture. Barak is mentioned only in Hebrews 11:32 where he is recognized for his faith. Why do you think Barak is mentioned but not Deborah?

_____
_____
_____
_____
_____

Study Note

1. Judges 4:16 states: "All the troops of Sisera fell by the sword, not a man was left." Most likely this was the sword of judgment, as Deborah explains in Judges 5:19-23 that God sent heavy rain that turned the Kishon River into a raging torrent. The chariots and horses would not have been able to move easily in the mud. Given the Canaanite god Baal was the god of storms, the sudden change in weather could have caused the superstitious Canaanites to think that Baal had turned against them. Clearly, the Canaanite god was no match for the God of Israel. It is no wonder that Sisera fled.

Reflections: God worked through Deborah to deliver the Israelites from the Canaanites. Was Deborah afraid? There is nothing in the passages to indicate that she was. God said go, and Deborah went! What Deborah started, Jael finished. Deborah's words to Barak in 4:9 came to pass: "Because of the way you are going about this, the honor will not be yours, for the Lord will hand Sisera over to a woman." Deborah is the only woman in the Bible to be a judge, a prophet, and a military leader. Now that's a courageous woman. #*Deuteronomy 20:1*

Week 3

A Noble Woman from a Foreign Land:
The Story of Ruth

Our next courageous woman is also from the period of the Judges, although the Scriptures do not tell us which judge was ruling Israel at the time. Unlike Rahab and Deborah, Ruth has an entire book dedicated to her story, but for the purposes of our study, we will focus on Ruth's character. Given we have already discussed the period of the Judges, just a brief history of Moab is all we need to get started.

As previously mentioned, the Moabites were one of the nations that oppressed Israel during the time of the Judges. But just who were the Moabites? Where did they come from? To answer these questions, we need to once again go back to the pages of Genesis, to the time of Abraham and his nephew Lot. The Moabites were descendants of Lot from his incestuous union with his eldest daughter (Genesis 19:30-38).

The Moabites occupied the land east of the Dead Sea in what is now Jordan. Numerous towns and villages were known to have existed there, as the land was very fertile. The Moabites possessed great military skill and were notorious raiders. They did not get along with the Israelites, and as a result, there were frequent battles.

The Moabites were not allowed to attend Israel's religious gatherings because they had refused to give the Israelites bread and water when they were in the desert after the Exodus (Deuteronomy 23:3-6). Further cruelty was demonstrated when the king of Moab called for curses to be invoked upon the Israelites (Numbers 22:1-6).

The Moabites worshiped many gods, such as Baal and Mot, but their chief deity was Chemosh (Numbers 21:29). Chemosh was a god of war, and as such, was expected to provide land for the Moabites through military conquests (Judges 11:24). To ensure victory, Chemosh required human sacrifices—usually children. One of the kings of Moab (Mesha) even offered his own son as a sacrifice to Chemosh in hopes of military victory (2 Kings 3:26-27).

Prostitution was also an integral part of Chemosh worship, known as "shrine prostitution." Sadly, the Israelite men indulged in sexual immorality with the Moabite women (Numbers 25:1-2) and began to serve the Moabite gods (Judges 10:6). It is understandable why God did not want the Israelites getting involved with the Moabites. Yet, the book of Ruth opens with an Israelite family moving from Bethlehem to Moab.

Please read Ruth Chapter 1.

1. What do we learn about Ruth from verses 1-7?

2. Naomi encourages Ruth to go home to her "people and her gods" (v. 15). What profound statement does Ruth make in verses 16 and 17?

3. Given the history between the Israelites and the Moabites, what type of reception might Ruth have anticipated upon arriving in Bethlehem?

4. After they arrived in Bethlehem, Ruth went to work gleaning barley in a field that belonged to a man named Boaz; and as it just so happened, Boaz was a relative of Naomi's late husband. When Boaz inquirers about Ruth, how does the foreman describe her in 2:6-7?

5. Boaz was very kind to Ruth. When Ruth asked Boaz why she had found favor in his eyes, how did Boaz respond in 2:11-12?

6. According to Israelite law, Boaz, being a relative of Naomi's late husband, could be their kinsman-redeemer. (See study note 1.) Naomi came up with a plan, and she sent Ruth to the threshing floor where Boaz was sleeping. When Boaz awoke, Ruth asked him to marry her and redeem her family (3:3-9). How did Boaz respond to Ruth's bold gesture in 3:10-11? (See study note 2.) Put yourself in Ruth's situation for just a moment. What do you think was going through her mind?

7. Ruth learned that there was a kinsman-redeemer nearer than Boaz; however, this man chose not to redeem, leaving the door wide open for Boaz (4:5-6). In the presence of witnesses, Boaz agreed to buy Naomi's land and marry Ruth. What blessing did the witnesses pray for Ruth in 3:11?

8. Ruth became Boaz's wife, and she gave birth to a son, Obed. What does 4:17 state about Obed's descendants? Read **Matthew 1:1-6** for further insight.

Study Notes

1. The book of Ruth connects two Israelite laws: kinsman-redeemer and levirate marriage. A kinsman-redeemer was a term for the near relative who was responsible for the economic well-being of a relative who was in personal or financial distress. The relative would serve as a redeemer of property and/or persons (Leviticus 25:47-55). Levirate marriage was an ancient Israelite custom, ordained by Moses, stating if a man died and did not have any children, his surviving brother was required to marry the widow in order to continue his brother's family through the son that might be born of that marriage. Another example of levirate marriage is found in Genesis 38:1-30.

2. In the NIV translation, Boaz describes Ruth as "a woman of noble character" (3:11). The original Hebrew word for noble is *hayil*, which means strength, capability, skill, valor, warrior, brave, valiant fighter.[4] Hayil is the same Hebrew word used to describe David in 1 Samuel 16:18: "He is a brave (*hayil*) man and warrior."

Reflections: Ruth had lost so much. She was a young widow. She left her home, her family, and all that was familiar to her, and she traveled to Bethlehem with her mother-in-law. As a foreigner, she did not know how she would be received; yet, she worked hard providing food for herself and for her mother-in-law. Ruth, a Moabite, faithfully followed Israelite law, and God blessed her. In looking at the genealogy of Jesus in Matthew 1:5, we notice a couple of fascinating points. First, Boaz was the son of a courageous woman, Rahab, and he married a courageous woman, Ruth. These women are two of only four women mentioned in the genealogy of Jesus, and none of these four women were Israelites! #*Isaiah 54:4*

---

4   Edward W. Goodrick and John R. Kohlenberger III, *The Strongest NIV Exhaustive Concordance* (Grand Rapids, MI: Zondervan, 1999).

Week 4

A Wise Woman in the Desert:
The Story of Abigail
(1 Samuel 25:1-44)

While the stories of Deborah and Ruth unfold during the period of the Judges, our next courageous woman is from the period of the monarchy. The Israelites decided that they wanted a king to lead them; after all, the other nations around them all had kings. They went to Samuel, Israel's final Judge, and demanded he appoint a king to lead them (1 Samuel 8:5, 19-20). Samuel prayed over their request, and God revealed to Samuel, "I will send you a man from the land of Benjamin. Anoint him leader over my people Israel" (1 Samuel 9:16). Samuel anointed Saul (10:1), and Saul was confirmed as Israel's first king (11:15). Saul, however, rebelled against God and deliberately disobeyed him (1 Samuel 13:9, 14:24, 15:9, 17-19). As a result, God rejected Saul as king (1 Samuel 15:26, 16:1).

The Lord then said to Samuel, "Fill your horn with oil and be on your way; I am sending you to Jesse of Bethlehem. I have chosen one of his sons to be king" (1 Samuel 16:1). Remember Jesse's name from our study of Ruth? Seven of Jesse's sons went before Samuel, but the Lord did not choose one of them (16:10). Finally, David, the youngest son, who had been out tending the sheep, was brought before Samuel. The Lord then told Samuel to anoint David, and "the Spirit of the Lord came upon David in power" (16:12-13). Even though Samuel had anointed David as king, Saul remained on the throne. In an attempt to secure his kingship, Saul pursued David with the intent to kill him. To escape Saul, David fled into the Desert of Maon. It was during his time in the desert that he met a young woman named Abigail—a woman who would have a profound impact on him.

Please read 1 Samuel 25:1-44.

1. Read 1 Samuel 25:1-3, and record everything you learn about Nabal and Abigail.

Nabal	Abigail

2. David and his men had protected Nabal's shepherds out in the fields. What did David request of Nabal in return and how did Nabal respond (v.v. 8-11)? (See study note for further insight.)

   _____
   _____
   _____
   _____
   _____

3. Clearly, David was angry. He was running from Saul; he was tired; and he was hungry. How did David respond to Nabal's words (v.v. 12-13; 22)?

4. When Nabal's servant told Abigail what had happened, what did Abigail do? Why do you think the servant went to Abigail?

5. According to 25:13, about four hundred men carrying swords were headed toward Nabal's house. Describe the scene in v.v. 20-22.

6. What profound words did Abigail say to David in v.v. 26-31, and what was David's response (v.v. 32-34)? Who exercised better judgment?

7. Read **Deuteronomy 32:35** and **Romans 12:19**. Whose place is it to avenge? What happened to Nabal? (Note the irony of David's greeting in 25:6.)

8. Clearly, David was impressed with Abigail's courage and wisdom. What did David ask of Abigail? Why do you think the author included the names of David's other wives? (Read **Deuteronomy 17:17** for further insight.)

Study Note

1. Both Nabal and David were from the tribe of Judah. David sought help in the form of food and water for himself and his men (25:11). David referred to himself as "your son David" (25:8), indicating the amicable relationship that David believed existed given that Nabal was his fellow kinsman. In 25:21, David was so angry that he no longer referred to Nabal as his father but as "this fellow."

Reflections: Take a moment to picture the scene: An angry David with four hundred of his men mount their horses and ride with swords drawn toward Nabal's house. Abigail courageously rides on her donkey toward David and his men, "armed" with some raisin cakes, loaves of bread, and wine! She made no excuses but simply apologized for what her foolish husband had done. Abigail successfully interceded on behalf of her evil husband and saved the lives of all those associated with her household. Abigail prevented David from seeking revenge and incurring God's judgment. She prophetically revealed to David that he would have a "lasting dynasty." David could have destroyed God's future plans for him if he had acted foolishly and not heeded Abigail's words. Now that's one wise and courageous lady! *#Jeremiah 1:8*

Week 5

An Unnamed Hero:
The Story of the Shunammite Woman
(2 Kings 4:8-37)

We have studied two women from the period of the Judges, and now we will look at our second woman from the period of the monarchy. All of the women we have studied so far have been identified in Scripture by name; this courageous woman, however, is not. Instead, she is identified by the town in which she lived. Once again, we need a little context to understand what is going on.

As we have already discussed, Saul was the first king of Israel, and he reigned for forty years (1 Samuel 13:1; Acts 13:21). After Saul's death, David assumed the throne. You may recall that David had already been anointed by Samuel (1 Samuel 16:12-13), and later the men of Judah anointed him as Israel's second king (2 Samuel 2:4). David would also reign for forty years, and after his death, his son Solomon became king (1 Kings 2:11-12). Like Saul and David before him, Solomon would reign for forty years (1 Kings 11:42).

Now, here is where it gets complicated. After Solomon's death, his son Rehoboam became king (1 Kings 11:43), but the northern tribes rebelled against Rehoboam because of the heavy taxes he had placed on them (1 Kings 12:4). The kingdom of Israel then divided. Ten tribes formed the Northern Kingdom and kept the name "Israel;" Samaria became its capital. Jeroboam, the son of Nebat, one of Solomon's officials, became the first king of the Northern Kingdom of Israel (1 Kings 12:20). The Southern Kingdom was formed by just two tribes: Judah and Benjamin. They took the name Judah, and Jerusalem was the capital. The Southern Kingdom of Judah remained loyal to the house of David and to King Rehoboam, the son of Solomon (1 Kings 12:21-24). Like I said, it's complicated.

The story of our next courageous lady, known only as the Shunammite woman, takes place during the reign of King Joram in the Northern Kingdom of Israel. She lived in the city of Shunem; hence, she was a Shunammite. In setting the stage for her story, it is important to keep in mind that the Northern Kingdom of Israel had rejected God. When the kingdom divided, King Jeroboam made two golden calves for his people to worship so that they would not go to the temple, which was located in Jerusalem, in the Southern Kingdom of Judah (1 Kings 12:28-30). Because of Israel's rebellion, God sent prophets to warn the kings and the people of the coming judgment if they did not repent. One of those prophets was a man named Elisha. Elisha would frequently pass through Shunem, and he developed a friendship with the Shunammite woman.

Please read 2 Kings 4:8-37.

1. What do we learn about the Shunammite woman in **2 Kings 4:8-10**? (See study note for further insight)

2. Elisha wanted to do something special for this woman because of her kindness. He asked his servant to inquire from her what she would like. How did she respond in verse 13? What do you think she meant by those words?

3. Gehazi notes that the woman did not have a son, and her husband was quite old. Elisha told her that at this time next year she would have a son. What was her response?

4. God fulfilled Elisha's promise to the woman, but tragically her son died. Her response is not what one would have expected. What did she do (v.v. 21-24)? Why do you think she told her husband, "It's all right"?

_____
_____
_____
_____
_____
_____

5. The woman traveled from her home in Shunem to Mount Carmel to see Elisha, a distance of about twenty miles. This was no easy journey on a donkey. Carefully read v.v. 25-28. Record the woman's words to Elisha's servant Gehazi, and then record her words to Elisha.

Woman's words to Gehazi	Woman's words to Elisha

6. Elisha sent Gehazi back to Shunem to place his staff "beside the boy's face," but the woman did not go with him. What did she say to Elisha and how did he respond in verse 30? What do you think her tone was?

7. Elisha returned to Shunem with the woman. He went to the child, whom the woman had placed in Elisha's room, and he prayed over him. What evidence does the Scripture provide to prove that Elisha had raised the boy to life?

8. How would you describe the Shunammite woman's faith and courage?

Study Note

1. Elisha never addressed this woman by name; he referred to her only as the *Shunammite* woman. Conversely, the woman never addressed Elisha by name but referred to him only as "the man of God" (2 Kings 4:9, 16, 21, 22, 25). The woman is identified by the city in which she lived: Shunem. Some eight hundred years later, in almost this exact location, a similar miracle would occur. By this time, the ancient city of Shunem would no longer exist. In the city of Nain, Jesus raised a widow's only son from the dead (Luke 7:11-17). Given that the *Shunammite's* husband was old (2 Kings 4:14), she might well have been a widow with an only son in the not too distant future. In the "widow of Nain" story, Jesus was referred to as a "great prophet" (Luke 7:16). Perhaps the people were associating Jesus with the ancient story of the Shunammite woman's only son.

Reflections: The Shunammite woman took action! When her precious son died, she got on her donkey and went straight to "the man of God." She knew that God had given Elisha power and that everything would be "all right," just as she had told her husband and Gehazi. She courageously told Elisha that she would not leave without him; in other words, she was not taking no for an answer. One can almost picture this woman standing there with one hand on her hip and the other hand pointing in the direction of Shunem, saying to Elisha, "You get yourself back to Shunem and fix this situation!" It would have been unheard of for a woman in that culture to take the steps that this woman took. She was a courageous woman of faith; an un-named hero of the Old Testament. *#John 14:27*

Week 6

A Courageous Queen:
The Story of Esther

The final courageous woman we will be studying on our journey through the Old Testament is Esther. Like Ruth, Esther has an entire book dedicated to her story. But once again, for the purposes of this study, we will focus on Esther's character and courage. As with the other courageous women we have studied, a little background is needed to set the stage.

We have already discussed that the nation of Israel divided into two kingdoms: Israel to the north and Judah to the south. Both of these kingdoms abandoned God and suffered judgment. The Northern Kingdom would only last for a little over two hundred years before falling to the Assyrians in 722 B.C. King Sargon II of Assyria deported the ten tribes, scattering them throughout the Assyrian Empire, and they disappeared from history. The Southern Kingdom lasted a little over three hundred years before falling to the Babylonians in 586 B.C. King Nebuchadnezzar of Babylon (in modern day Iraq) took many captives from Judah to Babylon to serve in his kingdom (2 Kings 24:14). The city of Jerusalem was left in ruins and the temple destroyed. The Jewish people remained in captivity for seventy years in what is known as the Jewish Exile (Jeremiah 25:11; 29:10). In 539 B.C., Cyrus the Great, king of Persia, conquered Babylon and allowed the Jewish exiles to return to Jerusalem and rebuild their city (Ezra 1:1-4). Some of the Jewish exiles chose to return, but many had become acclimated to the Persian culture and chose to stay.

The book of Esther tells the story of the Jewish people, who, about fifty years after Cyrus's decree, had chosen not to return to Jerusalem. The events in the book span a period of about ten years—483-473 B.C.—and fit historically between chapters 6 and 7 in the book of Ezra. The book of Esther opens with Xerxes, the king of Persia, throwing a lavish banquet for the nobles of the Persian Empire. King Xerxes was the son of Darius I and the grandson of Cyrus the Great. He had multiple wives and a large harem. King Xerxes' palace was located in Susa (in modern day Iran). The purpose of the banquet was to generate support and enthusiasm for his plan to invade Greece, an invasion that would turn out to be a complete failure. The partying continued, and on the seventh day, King Xerxes was "high in spirits from wine," and he demanded that his wife, Queen Vashti, be brought before him "wearing her royal crown in order to display her beauty to the peoples and nobles" (1:10-11). For whatever reason, Queen Vashti refused the drunk king's command, a behavior that would not have been tolerated in that culture. As a result, the publically humiliated king had Queen Vashti permanently banished. She would no longer be the queen. It would appear that King Xerxes could control everything but himself.

The banquet is over. The invasion of Greece, a failure. Time has passed, and King Xerxes misses his queen. The stage has now been set.

1. Read **Esther 2:1-23** and list what we learn about Esther (see study note 1 for further insight). In 2:10 the text states that Esther had not revealed her nationality because Mordecai had forbidden her to do so. Why do you think Mordecai gave this command?

   _____
   _____
   _____
   _____
   _____

2. The king promoted Haman to the second highest position in the empire. Everyone would bow down and honor Haman as he passed by—everyone

except Mordecai. Mordecai would bow down and worship God alone. What action did Haman take in 3:5-6?

3. Describe how Haman manipulated the king in 3:8-11. What exactly did the edict entail (3:13)?

4. Given that Esther was the queen, Mordecai reached out to her for help, but there was one problem: The king had not called for Esther in over thirty days, and anyone who approached the king without being summoned would be put to death (4:9-11). The only exception would be if the king extended his golden scepter to that person. How did Mordecai respond to Esther's predicament (4:13-14)?

5. Esther was clearly very isolated living in the harem. She had to communicate with Mordecai through another person, and she was completely unaware of the edict to annihilate her own people. How did Esther respond to Mordecai's request (4:15-16)? (See study note 2 for further insight.)

_____
_____
_____
_____
_____

6. After fasting and praying, Esther came up with a plan, and she approached the king, who extended his golden scepter. Given that Esther had risked her life to speak with him, the king must have known she had something very important on her mind. Knowing her husband loved a good party, Esther requested the first of two banquets to be attended by both the king and Haman. Why do you think Esther chose to have two banquets? At the second banquet, what did Esther reveal to the king (7:3-6)?

_____
_____
_____
_____
_____

7. How did Esther plan to save the lives of her people (8:5-11)?

_____
_____
_____
_____
_____

8. Given Esther's re-written edict (see study note 3), the Jewish people were able to defend themselves, and they were delivered from certain annihilation. Their "sorrow was turned into joy and their mourning into a day of celebration" (9:22). Esther's story is still celebrated today by the Jewish people. What is this celebration known as (9:23-32)?

_____
_____
_____
_____
_____

Study Notes

1. Esther was her Persian name, which means "star;" Hadassah was her Hebrew name, which means "myrtle." (It is interesting to note that the myrtle tree bears a flower that looks like a star). Esther 2:8 states that Esther was among the young girls "taken" into the king's harem. The Hebrew word translated as "taken" is *laqah*, which means to be led away, to be captured, taken away; seized.[5] This same Hebrew word *laqah* is used for Joseph when he was sold into slavery by his brothers and taken to Egypt in Genesis 39:1. These young girls did not volunteer; they had no choice. They were taken without regard for any plans they might have had for their futures. These young women would lose their virginity to a king who might never ask to see them again. If the king was no longer interested in a girl, she would just remain in the harem for the rest of her life with no chance for a real marriage and family. Hebrew scholar Michael V. Fox explains: "What is significant—and most oppressive—is that their will, whatever it may have been, is of no interest to anyone in the story. They are handed around, from home, to harem, to the king's bed. Their

---

5 *The Strongest NIV Exhaustive Concordance*, 4374

bodies belong to others, so much so that they are not even pictured as being forced. ... After their night with the king, they retired to the seraglio, still, of course, under the supervision of a eunuch, there to live out a plush but pointless imprisonment unless fetched once again."[6]

2. In the Old Testament, prayer always accompanied fasting: Exodus 34:28; Judges 20:26-27; Ezra 8:21-23; and 2 Chronicles 20:3.

3. Esther was able to neutralize Haman's previous edict, but she could not revoke it. In ancient culture, a royal decree or edict could not be repealed. This policy can also be seen in the book of Daniel 6:12-15. "It was not unreasonable for a monarch to refuse to rescind a law once publicly issued, for in doing so he would lose face and it would undermine his authority."[7]

Reflections: Esther went from being an orphan to the Queen of Persia to the woman who would save the Jewish people from annihilation. Wouldn't you love to know what Esther was thinking as she put on her royal robes and approached the king? Was she afraid? Was she thinking about God's covenant promises to Abraham and David and that somehow her people would be spared regardless of her fate? We don't know, but we do know that Esther was determined to do what needed to be done, even if she perished. Now that's one courageous lady! #Deuteronomy 31:6

We have looked at several courageous Old Testament women: Rahab, Deborah, Ruth, Abigail, the Shunammite woman, and Esther. Which courageous woman resonated with you the most? Why?

In the final two lessons of our study, we will take a look at some courageous women in the New Testament.

---

[6] Fox, Michael V., *Character and Ideology in the Book of Esther* (Eugene, OR: Wipf & Stock Publishers, 2010), p. 34, 35.

[7] Jobes, Karen H., *The NIV Application Commentary: Esther* (Grand Rapids, MI: Zondervan, 1999), p. 188.

Week 7

Mother of the Messiah:
The Story of Mary

The Old Testament closed with the Persian Empire firmly in control; however, in 331 B.C., the Persian Empire fell to Alexander the Great. The Greek Empire became the dominant world power, spanning three continents: Asia, Africa, and Europe. A major impact of Alexander the Great's conquest was the Hellenization of every land that he conquered and the assimilation of the people into the Greek culture. The Greek language became the official language throughout the empire. The Hebrew Old Testament was translated into Greek: the Septuagint. After the death of Alexander the Great, the sprawling Greek Empire was divided between his four generals. The constant fighting to gain more territory weakened the empire, and Rome began to increase in power. In 63 B.C., the Romans conquered Palestine, laying siege to Jerusalem and placing it under Roman control. The Greek Empire, which lasted about 269 years, had fallen to Rome.

The New Testament opens with the Roman Empire as the dominant world power. Antipater was appointed ruler of Judea and was later succeeded by his son, Herod the Great (37-4 B.C.). Israel was then divided into three regions: Galilee in the north, Samaria in the center, and Judea in the south. King Herod was a cruel, ruthless man who had several of his own sons and one of his wives killed because he believed they were a threat to his power. He was a shrewd politician and an oppressive leader. Herod was also a prolific builder, funding his numerous projects through heavy taxes, which resulted in severe financial burdens for the Israelites. There is no doubt that many Israelites paid half or more of all their wages in some form of tax.[8] One of Herod's most noteworthy projects was the rebuilding of the temple in Jerusalem. Although the temple would later be destroyed by the Romans in 70 A.D., the western retaining wall of the temple still stands and is known as Wailing Wall.

Our next courageous woman is Mary, and her story unfolds in Judea during the reign of King Herod.

---

8   Craig L. Blomberg, *Jesus and the Gospels* (Nashville, TN: Broadman & Holman Publishers, 1997), 61.

Please read Luke 1:26-38.

1. In verse 27, how is Mary described (note the order of Luke's words)? How did the angel Gabriel describe Mary in v. 28? (See study note for further insight.)

2. What was Mary's response to Gabriel's words in v.v. 29-30?

3. Gabriel told Mary that she would "be with child." List everything Mary was told about this child.

4. In your own words, explain how this child was going to be conceived.

5. How did Mary respond? Write out verse 38.

6. Given that Mary was not yet officially married to Joseph, what do you think she risked? Read **Deuteronomy 22:20-22** for further insight.

7. Keep in mind that Mary did not have to say yes to the angel; she could have refused. What if Mary had said no? Take a moment to reflect on this and record your thoughts.

8. Later, Mary would stand at the foot of the cross watching as her son died for the sins of this world—for her sins; for our sins (John 19:25). One can only imagine what she was thinking; the pain she was feeling. Yet, she stayed right there with her son. What does Mary's behavior tell you about her character?

___

Study Note

1. "Marriages were arranged for individuals by parents, and contracts were negotiated. After this was accomplished, the individuals were considered married and were called husband and wife. They did not, however, begin to live together. Instead, the woman continued to live with her parents and the man with his for one year. The waiting period was to demonstrate the faithfulness of the pledge of purity given concerning the bride. If she was found to be with child in this period, she obviously was not pure, but had been involved in an unfaithful sexual relationship. Therefore, the marriage could be annulled. … Mary and Joseph were in the one year waiting period when Mary was found to be with child."[9]

---

9   Walvoord, John F. and Roy B. Zuck, *The Bible Knowledge Commentary: New Testament* (Colorado Springs, CO: David C. Cook Publishers, 1983), p. 20.

Reflections: Notice that Mary did not hesitate. She did not say to the angel, "Let me think about it and get back to you," or, "I will discuss it with Joseph and let you know." No, Mary simply said yes. She knew she risked losing Joseph, the man she loved. She knew that at best, she would be the object of ridicule and scorn; at worst, she would lose her life! She would not have an easy road before her. An elderly man named Simeon would warn her: "A sword will pierce your own soul too" (Luke 2:25). Mary's grief would be like a sword piercing her soul. Yet, in spite of it all, Mary courageously stepped out in faith, and we are so thankful that she did! *#Luke 1:30*

Week 8

Courageous Women Who Walked with Jesus

The Bible states very little about Jesus' childhood. We are simply told that "the child grew and became strong; he was filled with wisdom, and the grace of God was upon him" (Luke 2:40). We are left to wonder what it was like for Mary and Joseph to raise the Son of God. In Luke 3:23, we are told that Jesus was about thirty years old when he began his ministry. The four Gospel writers, Matthew, Mark, Luke, and John, carefully recorded the events of Jesus' ministry, and throughout these Gospels, we see Jesus frequently interacting with women. He healed a woman who had been bleeding for twelve years (Matthew 9:20-22); He raised a young girl from the dead (Mark 5:22-43); He permitted a woman to sit in on his teachings (Luke 10:38-42); He ministered to a Samaritan woman (John 4:1-30); and He prevented a woman from being stoned to death (John 8:1-11), to name just a few. While these encounters might not seem shocking to us, we need to keep in mind the culture in which these women lived.

In his book, *Theology for the Community of God*, Stanley Grenz wrote: "Jesus transgressed the social norms of his day which prescribed the proper manner of treating women. In contrast to the rabbis and the Romans, he always related to women with highest respect. He not only defied social mores, he also destroyed religious custom, for he encouraged women to participate in areas reserved solely for men."[10]

---

10   Stanley J. Grenz, *Theology for the Community of God* (Grand Rapids, MI: William B. Eerdmans Publishing Company, 2000), 291.

This week we will take a look at some women who traveled with Jesus. Women who were with Jesus through it all: his ministry, his death, and his resurrection.

1. Read **Luke 8:1-3**. According to this passage, who was traveling with Jesus? (For further insight, see study note 1.)

2. What were these women doing? (For further insight, see study note 2.)

3. How do you think these women would have been regarded in their society?

4. Matthew 26:56 states that when Jesus was arrested in the Garden of Gethsemane, the disciples fled. Even Peter, one of Jesus' closest friends, denied knowing Jesus not once but three times (Mark 14:66-72). All of

these men deserted Jesus when he needed them the most. Read the four Gospel accounts of the crucifixion and record who stayed with Jesus as he suffered and died on the cross. Fill in the chart below.

Matthew 27:55-56	
Mark 15:40-41	
Luke 23:49	
John 19:25-27	

5. Given the situation, we can understand the disciples' fear, but what about these women? They served alongside Jesus too. Do you think their lives might have been in danger as well? (See study note 3 for further insight.)

6. The only disciple recorded as being at the cross with the women was John. What was Jesus concerned about in **John 19:26-27** as he hung on the cross?

7. Jesus spoke of his death and resurrection multiple times with the disciples, but it would appear that they did not understand.[11] According to the four Gospel accounts, who were the first to discover that the tomb was empty? Fill in the chart below.

Matthew 28:1-10	
Mark 16:9-11	
Luke 24:9-10	
John 20:1, 10-18	

8. Carefully reread **Matthew 28:5-8**. Who were the first to proclaim the Gospel message of the resurrection?

_____
_____
_____
_____
_____
_____

---

11   See Matthew 16:21, 17:22-23, 20:17-19; Mark 8:31, 10:32-34; Luke 9:21-22, 18:31-34.

Study Notes

1. Mary Magdalene "was the same Mary out of whom Jesus cast seven demons (Mark 16:9). The tradition that she had been an immoral woman before following Jesus is without any biblical support. The name Magdalene literally means 'from Magdala' and may refer to her hometown. The village of Magdala was on the Sea of Galilee about five miles north of the town of Tiberias."[12]

   "Joanna was apparently a woman of some status since her husband, Chuza, managed Herod's house. … There are unnamed women, unknown women, women with a broken past, and women of position. All kinds of women served the Lord and supported his ministry."[13]

2. The word translated as "support" in the NIV is the Greek word *diakoneo*, which means "to serve, help, attend to, to serve as a deacon; this often refers to spiritual and practical ministry in the Church."[14] It is the exact same word translated as "deacon" in 1 Timothy 3:10 where Paul describes the character of a deacon. These women were serving, ministering alongside Jesus and the disciples.

3. Throughout the book of Acts, there are many examples of persecution and suffering endured by the followers of Jesus: Stephen was stoned to death (Acts 7:54-60); James, one of Jesus' disciples, was beheaded (Acts 12:2); and the disciples as well as Paul and Silas were beaten, flogged, and imprisoned (Acts 5:17-18; 40; 16:22-24). But what about the women? In the last chapter of

---

12 Elmer Towns, *The Gospel of John: Believe and Live* (Chattanooga, TN: AMG Publishers, 2002), 200.

13 Thabiti Anyabwile, *Christ-Centered Exposition Exalting Jesus in Luke* (Nashville, TN: B&H Publishing Group, 2018), 143.

14 *The Strongest NIV Exhaustive Concordance*, 1354.

the book of Romans, the apostle Paul acknowledged many people, including women, who had helped him and who had faithfully served the Lord. Romans 16:3-4 states: "Greet Priscilla and Aquila, my fellow workers in Christ. They *risked their lives* for me." Unfortunately, Paul does not explain the incident he was referring to, but we do know that Aquila and Priscilla were husband and wife and they served with Paul (Acts 18:1-3). In Romans 16:7, Paul stated that Andronicus and Junias were in prison with him. Paul went on to say that "they (Andronicus and Junias) are outstanding among the apostles." Commentators believe that Andronicus and Junias were husband and wife. Theologian James Dunn explains: "The most natural way to read the two names within the phrase is as husband and wife. … We may firmly conclude, however, that one of the foundation apostles of Christianity was a woman and wife."[15] Based on these passages, women risked their lives and were imprisoned because of their faith in Jesus. Fast forward about 200 years, and the early church was still being severely persecuted. Theologian Bryan Litfin in his book, *Getting to Know the Church Fathers*, offers this insight: "Were there no women who contributed anything to early Christianity? The truth is there were many great women in the ancient church. We must remember that in ancient society, women rarely were taught to read and write, and certainly were not expected to produce an intellectual literary output. For this reason, few women's writings have come down to us today from the early church period. … To help keep this in mind, we will be looking at one of the few surviving ancient texts actually penned by a woman: the account of the noblewoman Perpetua, who went to her death by martyrdom in the year AD 203."[16] Perpetua and her handmaiden, Felicity, were imprisoned, tortured, and brutally executed in a public arena for their faith in Jesus Christ.

Reflections: These courageous women defied the social norms of their day and traveled with Jesus. They were the last ones at the cross and the first ones to the tomb. Were they ever afraid? Given the situation, quite possibly, but they were not going to let fear stop them. Like the other women we have studied, they knew God was with

---

15   James D.G. Dunn, *Word Biblical Commentary: Romans 9-16* (Dallas, TX: Word Books Publisher, 1988), 894, 895.

16   Bryan M. Litfin, *Getting to Know the Church Fathers* (Grand Rapids, MI: Brazos Press, 2007), 17.

them, and they stepped out in faith. It is important to keep in mind that Christianity stands or falls on the resurrection of Jesus. It is the very foundation of our faith; without it, we have nothing. Theologian Thabiti Anyabwile states that the resurrection of Jesus is "the greatest news story ever told."[17] What an honor that God entrusted his story, the Gospel message, the greatest news story ever told, to a group of women—a group of courageous women! *#Matthew 28:10*

---

17   Anyabwile, *Christ-Centered Exposition*, 354.

A Final Word

It's a wrap! These past eight weeks went by so quickly. We studied many women throughout the Bible who took the most frequent command in the Bible literally: "Do not be afraid." They stepped out in faith and are examples of God's words to Joshua, and indeed to us: "Be strong and courageous. Do not be afraid; do not be discouraged, for the Lord your God will be with you wherever you go" (Joshua 1:9). Amen!

#Passages

Week 1: Rahab: *#Deuteronomy 1:21* "See, the Lord your God has given you the land. Go up and take possession of it as the Lord, the God of your ancestors, told you. Do not be afraid; do not be discouraged."

Week 2: Deborah: *#Deuteronomy 20:1* "When you go to war against your enemies and see horses and chariots and an army greater than yours, do not be afraid of them, because the Lord your God, who brought you up out of Egypt, will be with you."

Week 3: Ruth: *#Isaiah 54:4* "Do not be afraid; you will not be put to shame. Do not fear disgrace; you will not be humiliated. You will forget the shame of your youth and remember no more the reproach of your widowhood."

Week 4: Abigail: *#Jeremiah 1:8* "Do not be afraid of them, for I am with you and will rescue you, declares the Lord."

Week 5: The Shunammite Woman: *#John 14:27* "Peace I leave with you; my peace I give you. I do not give to you as the world gives. Do not let your hearts be troubled and do not be afraid."

Week 6: Esther: *#Deuteronomy 31:6* "Be strong and courageous. Do not be afraid or terrified because of them, for the Lord your God goes with you; he will never leave you nor forsake you."

Week 7: Mary: *#Luke 1:30* "But the angel said to her, 'Do not be afraid, Mary; you have found favor with God.'"

Week 8: The Women Who Traveled with Jesus: *#Matthew 28:10* "Then Jesus said to them, 'Do not be afraid, Go and tell my brothers to go to Galilee; there they will see me."

Bibliography

Anyabwile, Thabiti. *Christ-Centered Exposition Exalting Jesus in Luke*. Nashville, TN: B&H Publishing Group, 2018.

Blomberg, Craig L. *Jesus and the Gospels*. Nashville, TN: Broadman & Holman Publishers, 1997.

Dunn, James D.G. *Word Biblical Commentary: Romans 9-16*. Dallas, TX: Word Books Publisher, 1988.

Fox, Michael V. *Character and Ideology in the Book of Esther*. Eugene, OR: Wipf & Stock Publishers, 2010.

Goodrick, Edward W. and John R. Kohlenberger III. *The Strongest NIV Exhaustive Concordance*. Grand Rapids, MI: Zondervan, 1999.

Grenz, Stanley J. *Theology for the Community of God*. Grand Rapids, MI: William B. Eerdmans Publishing Company, 2000.

Halley, Henry H. *Halley's Bible Handbook*. Grand Rapids, MI: Zondervan, 2000.

Jobes, Karen H. *The NIV Application Commentary: Esther*. Grand Rapids, MI: Zondervan, 1999.

Litfin, Bryan M. *Getting to Know the Church Fathers*. Grand Rapids, MI: Brazos Press, 2007.

Pressler, Carolyn. *Joshua, Judges, and Ruth*. Louisville, KY: Westminister John Knox Press, 2002.

Towns, Elmer. *The Gospel of John: Believe and Live*. Chattanooga, TN: AMG Publishers, 2002.

Walvoord, John F. and Roy B. Zuck. *The Bible Knowledge Commentary: New Testament*. Colorado Springs, CO: David C. Cook Publishers, 1983.

Wright, N. T. *Following Jesus: Biblical Reflections on Discipleship*. Grand Rapids, MI: William B. Eerdmans Publishing Company, 1994.

About the Author

Laura Noel graduated from Liberty University Willmington School of the Bible and has been involved with women's ministries for almost twenty years. She is also a registered nurse. Laura is married to the love of her life, Bill, and they reside in Texas. Laura and Bill have two grown children and an adorable miniature schnauzer. *God With Her: A Study of Courageous Women in the Bible* is her first book.

www.ingramcontent.com/pod-product-compliance
Lightning Source LLC
Chambersburg PA
CBHW081021040426
42444CB00014B/3306